Diets to help
COLITIS AND IRRITABLE
BOWEL SYNDROME

Colitis, or inflammation of the bowel, is a common ailment and this book shows how, with the correct dietary programme, the condition can be alleviated naturally. Irritable bowel syndrome (I.B.S.) can be similarly helped.

D0710954

Also in this series:

Diets to help

COLITIS AND IRRITABLE BOWEL SYNDROME

Natural relief with a carefully balanced regime

JOAN LAY
N.D., M.B.N.O.A.

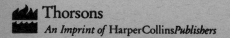

Thorsons
An Imprint of HarperCollins*Publishers*

Thorsons
An Imprint of HarperCollins*Publishers*
77–85 Fulham Palace Road,
Hammersmith, London W6 8JB

First published by Thorsons 1980 as *Diets to Help Colitis*
Repackaged 1988
This edition revised and updated 1995
10 9 8 7 6 5 4

A catalogue record for this book
is available from the British Library

ISBN 0 7225 3199 0

Printed and bound in Great Britain by
Caledonian International Book Manufacturing Ltd, Glasgow

Contents

Introduction

The word 'colitis' tends to be used rather inaccurately to include anything from a prolonged bout of simple diarrhoea – through mucous colitis to ulcerative colitis. The actual meaning is: 'inflammation of the colon'. The colon is the large intestine at the end of the digestive tract, where some absorption occurs, and the waste matter is moved on by muscular contractions at regular intervals (peristalsis).

Colitis is characterized, in its simplest form, by frequent watery stools of a forceful nature accompanied by low abdominal discomfort or pain commonly known as 'colic'. This stage is usually followed by a period of constipation until the colon is sufficiently irritated again to produce a violent effort once more to expel the waste matter in diarrhoea. The vicious circle continues in this way if nothing is done, or if suppressive measures are taken to stop the diarrhoea, until the body, in its effort to get rid of the continued pollution, uses even more drastic methods. The irritated mucous lining of the colon secretes excessively and is expelled with the stools in thready strings. This can continue for some time before the excessive activity of the mucous membrane actually causes the wall of the colon to become thinner. Then breakdown can occur and ulcerations form in small areas, and blood and pus can be seen in the stools.

During the past decade or so the phenomenon known as 'Irritable Bowel Syndrome' has been recognized. This is an exceptionally idiosyncratic condition and the symptoms are equally varied. Some are similar to those of colitis: gas, low abdominal pain, distention. Other symptoms include backache, general malaise, slight nausea, restlessness, lack of concentration and partial insomnia.

The standard treatments are all aimed at relieving symptoms, which temporarily make the patient more comfortable, but do not get at basic causes. The only satisfactory way of treating disease is in taking the person as an entire being, not divided up into compartments and labelled by symptoms. The patient can only be made healthy again by healthy or *whole* measures, using whole unprocessed foods, fresh air (when it can be found), water, exercise and right thinking. These very simple things can be assisted by vitamin, mineral and herbal supplements in the short run, but in the long run the way of living needs to be reviewed.

CHAPTER ONE

Causes of Colitis and Irritable Bowel Syndrome

COLITIS

The causes are numerous and varied, and each sufferer has his own unique pattern. Throughout all cases, however, there are certain factors that persistently appear, and these could be regarded as basic causes.

Digestion

Digestion begins in the mouth with the breaking-up of foods into small particles by thorough chewing and then the mixing of these particles with saliva. This facilitates swallowing and preparing the food to be worked on by the ferments in the stomach. Starch foods (cooked carbohydrates) actually begin being worked on in the mouth by enzymes in the ptyalin of the saliva. This first step is essential for good digestion, but it is interesting to note how many of the ordinary foodstuffs today are soft and bulkless. White bread can be chewed a little but before it is *thoroughly* broken up and mixed with the saliva it slides into the stomach incompletely prepared. The same thing occurs with puddings and cakes; even most cereals though crisp at first dissolve into a pappy mass when in contact with fluid and slide into the gullet all too easily. Overcooked vegetables and 'mash' are incompletely prepared and therefore the stomach enzymes cannot properly work on any of these foods. Digestion is slowed down, and fermentation occurs. The unconverted foodstuffs produce gas and this in turn causes distention, discomfort and 'heartburn' all lumped together under the umbrella of 'indigestion'.

All the foregoing phenomena result in nutritional loss because absorption is impaired. Energy is lost through more having to be expended on the effort to digest, so less is available to the muscles and brain, producing the tiredness and lack of concentration so often experienced with 'indigestion'. Then, in their turn, the intestines and colon suffer because the mineral and vitamin content of the food has been destroyed or not taken up owing to the gas and fermentation; and the lack of fibre and bulk in the food diminishes the stimulation to the gut and constipation ensues – setting up the vicious circle already mentioned.

Nervous and Emotional Stress

Stress causes blocking or inhibition of the sympathetic nerve plexuses, while exciting excessive secretion of adrenalin. This, in turn, upsets the rhythm and function of the digestive tract, so that all the processes of digestion, absorption and excretion become unbalanced.

It can be appreciated, then, how very important it is for sufferers to learn how to avoid stress and emotional turmoil, by relaxing, and thereby releasing the tensions. In addition, it is necessary to be *really* honest with oneself in trying to find out why one reacts with resentment, anger, or fear, and come to understand that a change of attitude is essential in helping the body to resume its normal balance. Revealing phrases often occur during consultation which show those reactions of resentment and fear. For example: 'I work my guts out for them.' or 'They would have the very stuffing out of you.'

It is not surprising that the sufferer centres his attention on the condition often counting the number of visits to the loo, and dwelling on the symptoms. Common reactions are fear of eating anything rough, or with pips, or 'acid'. Indeed, one is encouraged by orthodox advice, to keep to soft foods which tend to be devoid of any healing or nutritional properties. Body weight obviously goes down, and this only adds to the worry and fear. Certainly guidance is needed, and a qualified naturopath should be consulted.

Impoverished Refined Unbalanced Diet

There is a great deal of information available about diets of every sort, and, happily, the wholefood idea is spreading rapidly. Incorrect information and lack of understanding are also common, so a resumé here will be helpful.

The body cells have an inherent blueprint – or intelligence, to work to their optimum good, given the basic material to draw from. Therefore it follows that in illness something is amiss, the various body cells are not getting the necessary materials and become unbalanced or 'ill'.

Convenience foods, tinned, processed, dyed and flavoured foods are all unnatural, and not only rob the body of essential minerals, but add a burden of complicated chemicals, some of which may be positively harmful. It is really important to use simple foods, raw fruit and salads, whole grains, beans and pulses; nuts and natural dairy products. Those who eat meat should try to obtain free range poultry, and meat from animals unpolluted by growth hormones and concentrated feed. Some food and drink have a particularly depleting and irritating effect on the digestive tract as a whole. Such things as: coffee and tea; chocolate and sugar; spices and pickles and condiments; alcohol and nicotine (from smoking); also mucous-forming foods like milk, cheese and refined white flour products (bread, biscuits, cakes etc.).

It stands to reason that if the diet is not balanced, the body will suffer. Indeed the whole body will be under par, and coupled with the stress factor already mentioned, and the emotional state of the patient in question, the imbalance will result in diarrhoea, then constipation and, eventually, colitis.

Regular Use of Strong Laxatives

This inevitably follows on from the above. The lack of fibre in the diet, which acts as a natural stimulant to the lining of the colon, and encourages the reflex defecation, results in a sluggish bowel. Particularly so because the whole digestive tract is depleted, missing the good whole unrefined foods necessary for good health. Therefore the automatic urge to defecate is missing (or very weak and so ignored) the waste matter will remain in the lower bowel unexpelled and this can persist for several days until, suddenly realizing the lack of elimination, the patient resorts to a laxative of some sort. Most of these are harsh, causing a 'scouring' effect on the bowel and therefore an extreme reaction in the mucous lining of the tract, which can be so severe that diarrhoea persists for a few days. This is followed by exhaustion in the area after so much activity, constipation recurs, and the whole cycle is set up again.

Prescribed drugs

Some of these, particularly the antibiotics and sulphonamides, inhibit the natural action of the intestinal flora and even destroy these *beneficial* bacteria. Their action in the normal way is to ingest the poisonous wastes in the faecal mass and render them harmless, so if they are destroyed the colon becomes unhealthy and a state of autotoxaemia is produced. Nature's method of trying to eliminate these wastes is increased secretion of mucous in the area. There is also a fall in the prothrombin content of the blood and a nicotinic acid deficiency. As a result the vessel walls are weakened and there is an increased risk of bleeding. Therefore a colitis can be a side-effect, of drugs prescribed for some other condition.

Allergy

The most common foodstuffs that react on the digestive tract to cause symptoms of diarrhoea and flatulence are milk, fats and gluten. The latter, a nitrogenous part of the starch of wheat, oats, barley and rye, causes a condition known as 'coeliac illness' or 'malabsorption syndrome'. This, however, a subject on its own; though it could be mistaken for colitis.

I.B.S.

The causes of colitis described above can apply to I.B.S. as well. The following factors, additionally, can contribute to the development of I.B.S.:

- Pressure of work – the ambition factor, the urge to 'get on'.
- Keeping irregular hours – eating at different times, eating in transit, missing meals; eating snacks and junk food.
- Overeating – bloating the gut, regular intakes of spicy foods, such as chilli and curry, and fried food.
- Surgical operations – especially those involving abdominal interference.
- Trauma – falls, especially those affecting the lower back.

CHAPTER TWO

Outline of the Diet

PREPARATION – REST AND POSITIVE THINKING

Rest is important at the beginning of any radical change in regime, so that the body's energies can be concentrated in its effort to normalize and heal. In the cause of colitis, where great fatigue and dehydration occur, this is essential. The change of diet will be utilized more fully, and any adverse reactions to it lessened after a period of rest and relaxation. To start with, two days in bed, followed by five easy days will provide a break in the usual routine and relief from the usual daily pressures. This will provide a firm basis for recovery.

It would obviously be a waste of time to try this new way of living if one is plagued by doubts and fears about the outcome. One needs to be as positive as possible, accepting the fact that there are bound to be variations in progress.

Calmness and confidence are all-important, remembering that over-stimulation of the system by excitement or worry causes an immediate reaction from the colon and brings on the symptoms.

BREATHING

Once the decision is made to follow this method, the first thing to learn is how to breathe properly. Though this is not a dietetic factor – no diet, however balanced, can be fully effective if breathing is shallow, because the blood stream will not be properly oxygenated and so all functions will be less efficient. In addition, it is through deep slow breathing that relaxation is learnt; and as was stated at the beginning, this is an essential part of the treatment to relieve the emotional stress and tension. A third point, to emphasize the benefit obtained from using the diaphragm properly, is that its mechanical movement in rising and falling exerts slight pressure on the gut, and works as a sort of internal massage. This is valuable in restoring tone and rhythm to the large intestine.

How is it done? Lie comfortably on the back with a small pillow beneath the head, and a larger one beneath the thighs for support. Place both hands lightly on the abdomen over the navel. 'Think' the breathing into this area – then gently and slowly inhale and feel the abdomen swelling up under the hands; exhale, and the abdomen sinks down. At first, the ribs may expand as usual and the chest heave up, while the abdomen flattens – the old breathing pattern in fact. To overcome this, voluntarily push the abdominal muscles up when inhaling, and let them go on exhaling and gradually the different feeling will be experienced. A good time to practice is on waking and just before going to sleep. Six breaths is all that is needed, and then forget the special technique until the specified time. Remember not to get too involved and worry about it, or the good result will be defeated. Regular practice is the thing and the new rhythm will gradually take over – and if there is an occasion to cause anxiety – then a few diaphragmatic breaths will ease the 'butterflies', and in time, deep breathing can and will prevent these feelings.

NECESSARY NUTRIENTS

What particularly do those with colitis and I.B.S. need? The impoverished gut cannot at once cope with the roughage of raw foods, and to attempt to eat them would cause a very violent reaction. Slow re-education is the best way. The body really needs a vitamin and mineral rich source of nourishment to begin to redress the imbalance and encourage the arousal of the inherent healing power of the body. To do this without the roughage, at first means using vegetable and fruit juices, progressing to gentle bulk such as that in ripe bananas, brown rice and blended or liquidized fruit and vegetables.

The whole digestive tract may be so sensitive that cooked fruit and vegetables may have to be used initially; for example, steamed carrots and beetroots, baked and stewed apples and so on. The pectin of apples is very beneficial.

It cannot be emphasized too much that all the refined,

irritating and harmful foods and drinks *must* be deleted and recognized as being not only useless but a definite hindrance to good health. They should not feature again in the diet, even after the condition has been cured.

The curative regime needs to be rich in all the B vitamins to nourish the nervous system; in vitamin C to improve absorption of iron and the health of the blood vessels; in vitamin P to improve the healthy function of the mucous membranes. The minerals particularly needed are iron, magnesium, potassium and zinc. To provide these essentials, foods rich in vitamin B are: soya, brown rice, hazel and peanuts, millet, lentils, whole grains, liver, sesame seeds. Vitamin C is to be found in citrus fruits, peppers, blackcurrants, parsley, raw vegetables, salads and fruits, sprouted seeds; vitamin P in the cells and pith of citrus fruits – so it is important to eat the flesh of the fruit as soon as one is acclimatized to take it. The minerals can be provided by molasses, grapes and raisins, green leafy vegetables, dried fruits and sunflower seeds. The list could be made longer, but these are some of the important sources. In addition natural, 'live' yogurt will be necessary to re-establish the intestinal flora, and garlic to act as a mucus solvent and antiseptic.

BALANCED MEALS

It is also advisable not to have too many mixtures of foods at one meal because at best, something is imperfectly digested, tending to produce gases and therefore distension and discomfort. It is better not to mix starches and fruits or starches and animal proteins – the acids in both fruit and meat work on the starches causing fermentation and therefore gases, distension, 'rumblings' and discomfort.

The best combinations are: fresh and dried fruits; nuts; milk; salads with starch (bread or potatoes) or salads with protein (egg, cheese, nuts); animal protein with green vegetables; vegetable protein with green vegetables.

When the digestive tract is very upset, as in this condition, it is better to have only one course – as much as is needed – without following it with a 'sweet'.

Many people with colitis are very concerned about weight loss, and the cleansing period of two to four weeks on a very restricted intake is the chief block in adopting a Nature Cure regime. It must be understood that however much one 'feeds up' while the colon is inflamed and generally unhealthy, proper absorption cannot take place. Whereas a properly supervised light diet can and does produce, after a time, the gain in weight they so much desire.

SUPERVISION

This book will be read by some who are trying to 'go it alone' but it is far better, both because of the stress factor and for more lasting results, to have the advice and support of a qualified naturopath.

Ideally, a few days on water only, then on juices only,

would be the way to begin the recuperative process; but this should *not* be tried unless there is the supervision mentioned above. The plan detailed later will be just as effective, but will take longer in producing tangible results. In either case the patient should think in terms of months rather than weeks. After all, the condition is the result of prolonged faulty living, and re-education is not a quick process.

NOTES FOR FOLLOWING THE CLEANSING PROGRAMME

1 Tap-water is heavily chlorinated and boiling removes this. In areas where sodium fluoride has been added to the main supply, bottled water would be better. There are several types available in supermarkets and wine shops – some still and some sparkling – either will do, providing it is natural spring water. The use of boiled or bottled water simply removes possible irritants and when full recovery is made need not be continued unless there is a preference to do so.

2 Too much salt is irritating and hardening but, as much of the body's salts are lost through the frequent stools, a very little, say a quarter of teaspoonful, may be added to the water when boiling rice. To make it more appetizing a little finely chopped fresh mint can be added, or parsley which is rich in vitamin C.

3 To make carrot juice without an extractor spread a sheet of gauze over a soup plate. Use the fine side of the grater and grate two medium carrots (having scrubbed them) into this cloth – gather it up by the edges so that the carrot pulp is in a bag – then gently twist and squeeze out all the juice. Pour this into a glass and drink at once, though slowly, before the vitamins and minerals become oxidized.

4 Always eat and drink slowly, savouring the food, chew very well and think about the source of the food – how much it has developed from earth, water, sun, and has concentrated these elements to feed your body.

5 Food should not be eaten very hot, as it overstimulates.

6 Two or three deep breaths before eating releases tension in the solar plexus (the area in the midriff where one feels 'butterflies' if anxious).

7 When following the day to day plan, only progress if there has been no marked reaction. If there is a temporary increase in diarrhoea keep the same diet for another day until it subsides.

8 Brown rice is recommended for all bowel irregularities because it provides bulk, traces of B-vitamins and very soft fibre.

9 Apples, cooked, raw or juiced, contain pectin, which helps to 'bind' or 'set' the too-fluid content of the descending colon (plus vitamin C, which helps to balance digestion).

10 Live yogurt provides the acidophilus bacteria destroyed by frequent purging and some drug

treatments, and re-establishes the intestinal flora necessary for health. (If it is found to be too 'sour' to take, a small amount of honey should be added.)

11 Bananas should be really ripe, as the sugars and starches are then fully developed and easily digested and absorbed.

12 Slippery elm food prepared from a special tree-bark is extremely soothing and beneficial to the gut. Biobalm is equally good in this respect.

13 Yeast and wheat and products that contain them should be *avoided* by the I.B.S. sufferer – at least for a month or two. Ryvita, rice and oat cakes can be substituted for wheat bread.

14 Marigold Bouillon Powder may be used either made up as a hot drink or sprinkled over rice or vegetables instead of yeast extracts.

15 Fruit juices of 4 fl.oz.

CHAPTER THREE

Cleansing and Healing Programme

Resting in bed.

1st day

7am Half-tumbler of cooled boiled water or bottled water, sipped slowly

8am 2 tablespoonsful of boiled brown rice with 1 level tablespoonful of stewed apple with honey

10am Boiled or bottled water as before

12 noon Brown rice and apple as at 8am

2pm Juice from two carrots

4pm Brown rice and apple

6pm Boiled or bottled water

8pm Slippery elm food (follow instructions on packet)

10pm Water plus pure red grape juice (2 fl. oz or 50ml of each)

2nd day

Repeat – still resting.

3rd day

Repeat, but at 10am have juice from 2 carrots instead

4th day
One may, at this stage, be out of bed but taking it easy.
Repeat the same diet as for day 3.

5th day
7am Water
8am One ripe banana, (or soaked dried banana); 1
    tablespoonful of brown rice
10am Carrot juice
12 noon 2 tablespoonsful (heaped) of boiled brown rice
    with ½ teaspoonful of Bouillon powder sprinkled over
    and 1 level tablespoonful of finely grated raw carrot
2pm Apple juice
4pm 1 banana with rice
6pm Camomile tea
8pm Slippery elm food or Biobalm
10pm Grape juice with only 1 tablespoon water

6th day
Repeat

7th day
Same, but take *neat* grape juice at 10pm

8th day
7am Water
8am 2 tablespoonsful of stewed apple with 1 level
    tablespoonful of ground almonds
10am Carrot juice
12 noon 3 tablespoonsful of brown rice with ½ tea-
    spoonful of Bouillon powder, 2 tablespoonsful of

carrot finely grated, plus ½ tablespoonful of finely chopped parsley

2pm Apple juice

4pm 2 soaked dried bananas

6pm Camomile tea

8pm Slippery elm food

10pm Grape juice

9th day
Repeat 8th day.

10th day

7am Apple juice

8am Grated raw apple with 1 tablespoonful ground almonds

10am Carrot juice

12 noon 3 tablespoonsful of brown rice with Bouillon powder, 2 tablespoonsful of grated carrot, ½ table-spoonful chopped parsley, 1 teaspoonful of sunflower seeds

2pm Half an orange to be eaten segment by segment

4pm 2 soaked dried bananas plus 1 tablespoonful of ground almonds

6pm Camomile tea

8pm Baked apple with honey, slippery elm food

10pm Grape juice

11th day

7am Apple juice

8am Fresh banana and ground almonds

10am Carrot juice

12 noon Small salad of: grated carrot, grated apple, chopped parsley, sunflower seeds, scalded and skinned tomato and 1 tablespoon of cottage cheese

2pm Eat half orange or grapefruit

4pm 2–3 steamed carrots (according to size) with 1 tablespoonful of cottage cheese

6pm China tea or camomile

8pm Baked apple and honey, slippery elm food

10pm Grape juice

12th day
Repeat

13th day

7am Apple juice

8am Grated apple plus 2 tablespoonsful of natural yogurt (honey if needed)

10am Carrot juice

12 noon Small salad as before, but add 2-3 lettuce leaves

2pm Half orange or grapefruit

4pm 2 steamed potatoes in their skins (remove skin before eating) plus 2 tablespoonsful of steamed cabbage and 2 tablespoonsful of cottage cheese

6pm China or camomile tea

8pm 1 baked apple and slippery elm food

10pm Grape juice

14th day
Repeat

End of strict cleansing and healing programme. At this stage the patient may be tempted to give up; either because improvement makes him feel secure and it has all been easy, or because problems have arisen and the setbacks due to the changed habits depress him, and make him feel that nothing will help.

It would be a great mistake to discontinue now – improvement must be maintained in order to re-educate the entire digestive tract thoroughly. Years have been spent in producing the condition, therefore months will be necessary to remove it. It would be wrong to regard the regime as a 'cure'; it should be appreciated as a new way of living, and that by this revision much will be prevented from going wrong in future. Indeed, a new dimension will be added to life by a realization of well-being and harmony because the body is reacting to the balance and wholeness of the diet and functioning at a higher level. Gradually, greater energy will be found; greater ability to cope with problems because the whole attitude has changed to being positive and constructive.

CHAPTER FOUR

Third and Fourth Week Diet

After the strict regime some improvement will be noticed, but it is advisable to proceed slowly. The third week can be spent in altering the pattern by resuming three meals a day with drinks in between, remembering that one may drink half an hour before a meal but not less than two hours after a meal.

It would be helpful to increase the rather limited salad to include lettuce, cress and some finely chopped or sliced red and/or green pepper – these are very rich in vitamin C. One slice of a hundred per cent wholewheat bread can be taken with this meal with a good margarine or unsalted butter. This will provide some of the B vitamins.

It would be as well to alter one meal at a time, or the stimulus to the digestive tract would be too great at this stage; so the whole week should centre on expanding the lunch little by little, and keeping two days the same before adding something new. If flatulence or diarrhoea occurs, lessen the amount of the new foodstuff until it is tolerated; should there still be a reaction, delete that food, and it can be used later when the tract has become less sensitive. Remember to keep a high resolve, and not to get depressed or thrown off course when such a reaction occurs.

Presuming that all has gone to plan in the third week, the fourth week should be used to develop the evening meal. Millet and soya savouries can be tried. Pasta dishes (brown of course) and lentil savouries. Examples of these are given later in the recipe pages. In addition, the green vegetable content of the meal should be varied and more adventurous, omitting those that are known to cause flatulence: onions, cauliflower, peas, parsnips and turnips. Overcooked brussel sprouts will also be most indigestible. Indeed, it is interesting to note that any *overcooked* vegetable, especially the green variety, can even cause flatulence in those without a digestive problem.

Lightly cooked liver may be included if liked, as it is easily broken down and is a rich source of iron and B vitamins. Chicken (if free-range and unpolluted by hormones) and fish (cod, haddock, plaice; but *not* the rich ones – halibut, salmon, trout, mackerel – or the so-called 'smoked' ones) can be served once a week also if the patient is non-vegetarian. However, the writer will continue on vegetarian diet reform lines. It is of course understood that frying is absolutely out of the question as a method of cooking anything.

The following menus are intended only as guide. It may be found preferable to remain on the same one for three, even four days; but the ones given do provide an idea of how the dietetic progression should be made.

MAINTENANCE MENUS
Menu 1 (days 1 and 2)

First thing: 4 oz (100g) apple juice

Breakfast: 1 grated raw apple (including skin and core)
   1 tablespoonful of soaked raisins
   1 tablespoonful of natural yogurt

Mid-morning: 4 oz (100g) of carrots, juiced

Lunch: Salad with small amounts of: lettuce, skinned
   tomato, grated carrot, sunflower seeds (heaped
   teaspoonful), grated raw beetroot, 2 oz (50g) cottage
   cheese

Mid-afternoon: China tea or herb tea

Evening meal: 1 or 2 steamed potatoes and carrots
   according to size
   1–2 tablespoonsful of steamed and chopped cabbage
   with poached egg

Bedtime: 4 oz (100g) red grape juice warmed or cold

The patient should eat enough to satisfy, but not to feel
full up. Main course only, without a sweet, will be the
pattern for some time yet.

N.B. Each menu to be repeated the following day.

Menu 2 (days 3 and 4)

First thing: Half tumbler hot water with teaspoonful of
   honey and slice of lemon

Breakfast: 2-3 soaked dried bananas, 2 tablespoonsful
   of natural yogurt

Mid-morning: 4 oz (100g) of carrots, juiced

Lunch: Salad with small amounts of: lettuce, cress, pepper, grated carrot, sunflower seeds, skinned tomato, 2 oz (50g) ground almonds, 1 slice of wholewheat bread and butter or Ryvita.

Mid-afternoon: China tea, herb tea or apple or grape juice

Evening meal: Savoury millet, 1 or 2 carrots, 1 or 2 tablespoonsful of green vegetable

Bedtime: Red grape juice or 'Vecon'

Menu 3 (days 5 and 6)

First thing: Half tumbler hot water with juice of ½ lemon plus 1 teaspoonful of honey

Breakfast: Soya or barley flake 'porridge' with soaked raisins and skimmed milk

Mid-morning: 'Vecon' or carrot juice or Bouillon

Lunch: Salad with small amounts of: lettuce, cress, skinned tomato, pepper, sunflower seeds, grated raw beetroot, 3 oz (75g) cottage cheese, 1 jacket potato medium size

Mid-afternoon: Soya savoury with carrots, cabbage, boiled beetroot (skinned when cooked)

Bedtime: Red grape juice or 'Vecon' or Bouillon

N.B. When beetroot has been eaten in any quantity, stools and urine may appear pinkish red – quite normal, so do not be alarmed!

Menu 4 (days 7 and 8)

First thing: Lemon and honey drink or apple juice

Breakfast: Raw apple, fresh banana, yogurt – amounts as suitable

Mid-morning: 1 teaspoonful of molasses in warm water – or eaten off the spoon with water to follow

Lunch: Salad as usual with *either* baked potato *or* 1 slice rye or wholewheat bread and butter. 2 oz (50g) milled nuts or 2-3 oz. (50-75g) cottage cheese and chopped parsley

Mid-afternoon: China tea, or camomile herb tea, apple or grape juice

Evening meal: Brown spaghetti with tomato sauce, carrots, runner beans (in season) or greens of some sort

Bedtime: Bouillon (1 teaspoonful to a cup of boiled water) or red grape juice

Menu 5 (days 9 and 10)

First thing: Lemon and honey drink as before

Breakfast: Grated raw apple, tablespoonful ground almonds, 2 tablespoonsful of soaked raisins

Mid-morning: Molasses as before

Lunch: Salad as usual with either potato or bread, and try 1-2 oz (25-50g) grated Cheddar or Cheshire cheese

Mid-afternoon: As usual

Evening meal: Herb almond pudding with carrots, peas and green vegetable

Bedtime: Bouillon or red grape juice

Menu 6 (days 11 and 12)

First thing: Lemon and honey or juice of half fresh grapefruit
Breakfast: A few Bran flakes, fresh banana, dried skimmed milk
Mid-morning: Molasses and apple juice
Lunch: Salad with bread or potato and 1 hard boiled egg
Mid-afternoon: As usual – tea or fruit juice
Evening meal: Rice savoury, carrots, tomatoes, green vegetable
Sweet: Yogurt and honey
Bedtime: Bouillon or grape juice

N.B. Have bread or potato at lunch on alternate days, i.e. do not just keep to one type of starch because you happen to prefer it. Try rye bread.

Menu 7 (days 13 and 14)

First thing: Apple juice
Breakfast: Half a grapefruit, 8-12 grapes, 1 apple, natural yogurt and honey
Mid-morning: Bouillon or molasses
Lunch: Salad with added dried raisins, 2-3 oz. (50-75g) Cheshire, Lancashire or Cheddar cheese
Mid-afternoon: As usual tea or fruit juice
Evening meal: Bean savoury, carrots, green vegetable
Sweet: Baked apple and honey
Bedtime: Bouillon or grape juice

One month has now been completed, the patient will feel more secure, more energetic and will have gained one to four pounds in weight.

In the event of a recurrence of symptoms it would be advisable to return to the strict regime for a few days.

MAINTENANCE RECIPES
Brown (whole) Rice

3 tablespoonsful washed brown rice
½ pint (275ml) water
¼ teaspoonful of salt
1 teaspoonful of sunflower seed oil

Bring water, salt and oil to the boil, add washed rice and stir. Bring back to boil, cover and lower heat. Simmer 35-40 minutes or until water absorbed. This yields 6 tablespoonsful of cooked rice. (All tablespoons are level.)

Flavourings
Finely chopped mint
Finely chopped parsley
Bouillon powder
Oregano
Sage
Honey
Grated lemon rind

For the above amount of rice
1 teaspoonful of fresh herbs
½ teaspoonful of dried herbs

1 teaspoonful honey
½ teaspoonful lemon rind

Stewed Apple

Use Bramley cooking apples with a small amount of water to simmer, and honey to taste – but under-sweeten in preference.

Apple Juice

It is better to use freshly made apple juice, but a good brand of bottled juice is all right, especially first thing in the morning. Remember to have fresh juice sometimes.

Soaked Raisins

Wash raisins well. Supermarket ones are soaked in mineral oil (liquid paraffin) to make them look glossy and weigh heavier. These need to be washed under running warm water and stirred around. When clean, put into a heat-proof bowl or basin, add a strip or two of lemon rind, then pour on boiling water just to cover them. Leave to soak overnight and they will be ready for the morning.
N.B. Always be sure to chew these raisins really well.

Salad Dressings

(1)
2 tablespoonsful of sunflower seed oil

1 tablespoonful of lemon juice
1 teaspoonful of honey
Put all into a bottle, screw on lid, and shake

(2)
1 tablespoonful of oil
1 tablespoonful of lemon juice
2 tablespoonsful of natural yogurt
1 teaspoonful of honey
Mix in same way

Dried Bananas

(from health food shops). These will not need washing
– so proceed as for raisins.

Savoury Millet (1–2 servings)

1 clove garlic
3 tomatoes
1 level teaspoonful of Bouillon powder
½ pint (275ml) water
1 teaspoonful of chopped, fresh parsley
2 tablespoonsful of millet

Skin and slice tomatoes and put into a pan with water,
crushed garlic and bouillon. Bring to the boil, sprinkle
in the millet and stir well. Cover and simmer for 10-15
minutes – liquor should be absorbed, but cook a few
minutes longer if still 'soupy', stirring. Serve as soon as
dry enough. Sprinkle on the fresh parsley.

Soya and Barley Flakes

(from health food shops). Instructions for making porridge is on the packet. Generally: 1 cupful of flakes to 2 cupsful of water, simmer for 15-20 minutes.
N.B. These flakes are useful in savouries and soups.

Soya Savoury

Prepared soya chunks or mince can be obtained at health food shops. Get the natural, unflavoured variety. Reconstitute the soya in liquor flavoured with bouillon and crushed garlic. Follow instructions given, deleting onion at present – grated raw carrot added at beginning of cooking helps to flavour, and also skinned tomatoes (same as for millet).

Bean Savoury

Use adzuki beans – small brown beans. These should be soaked either overnight or for 3-4 hours before using. Pour off the soaking water. Add fresh made up bouillon to cook:

3 tablespoonsful of adzuki beans, soaked
2 cloves crushed garlic
2 skinned tomatoes
½ pint (275ml) bouillon
1 teaspoonful of honey
1 tablespoonful of lemon juice

Simmer all together for 1 hour until the liquor is all absorbed. Serve.

Rice Savoury

2 tablespoonsful of brown rice
1 teaspoonful of oil
1 pint (500ml) boiling water and a little salt

Boil rice for 25 minutes, strain and rinse under hot water. Return to pan, add:

1 crushed clove garlic
1 tablespoonful chopped fresh parsley
½ teaspoonful mixed herbs
½ grated apple
1 tablespoonful of sunflower oil
½ cup boiling water

Cover and shake pan while cooking for a further 15 minutes. Serve.

Herb Almond Pudding

2 tablespoonsful of wholewheat breadcrumbs
2 tablespoonsful of ground almonds
1 teaspoonful of mixed herbs
1 tablespoonful of chopped parsley
1 egg
1 cupful of made up Bouillon

Mix dry ingredients, beat egg in ½ cupful of liquor and add to dry ingredients. Beat well and use up rest of liquor to make a stiff batter. *Either* put into greased basin, cover and steam for 45 minutes *or* put into greased baking dish and bake at 375°F (191°C, Gas mark 4) for 25 minutes.

Brown Spaghetti

(from health food shops). Cook as instructed on packet.

Tomato Sauce

3 skinned tomatoes
1 clove crushed garlic
1 teaspoonful of honey
1 tablespoonful of oil
½ cupful of water

Cook all together for 10 minutes. If preferred thicker, add 2 teaspoonsful of brown rice flour sprinkled on and cook for 3–5 minutes more.

CHAPTER FIVE

Progressive Diet

The diet can now assume normal lines. That is to say, of course, normal diet reform lines. The menus will be vegetarian, but meat, fish or poultry will be indicated in brackets for those feeling the need for flesh foods.

It is to be hoped that the improvement reached, so far, will be maintained without set-backs. There is no reason to expect them if one can maintain a relaxed unemotional and positive outlook, while enjoying life both at work and at home. There are bound to be problems and disagreements, but if these are coped with without suppressing them and 'bottling up' feelings, no reaction in the gut will occur; particularly now that the whole area has been renewed in healthy activity.

Where a choice is indicated on the menu, it is obviously better to vary your choice – the balance would be better with a variety. Though, to have two or three days on the same thing for economy's sake would be allowable.

PROGRESSIVE MENUS
Menu 1

First thing: (choice of)
Lemon and honey
Bottled apple juice
Bottled water

Breakfast: ½ grapefruit
8-12 grapes
1 apple
Yogurt (natural)

Mid-morning: (choice of)
Tomato juice
Grapefruit juice
Bouillon
Carrot juice
Grape juice

Lunch: Salad: Lettuce, water cress, pepper, tomato,
grated carrot grated beetroot, few raisins; 2 oz (50g)
milled nuts, sunflower seeds
One baked potato
Baked apple to follow

Mid-afternoon: China tea or herb tea

Evening meal: Casserole of vegetables (grilled chop),
carrots, cabbage and boiled rice
4-6 soaked prunes to follow

Bedtime: Grape juice, slippery elm or bouillon

Menu 2

First thing: (choice of):
Lemon and honey
Bottle apple juice
Bottled water

Breakfast: 1 boiled egg
2 slices 100% wholewheat bread with butter (unsalted)
   or Ryvita
1 apple

Mid-morning: (choice of):
Bouillon
Grapefruit juice
Carrot juice
Grape juice

Lunch: Salad: Lettuce, pepper, tomato, grated carrot,
   grated apple, sunflower seeds 4 oz (100g) cottage
   cheese
1 slice 100% wholewheat bread with butter or Ryvita
Soaked raisins and yogurt

Mid-afternoon: China tea or herb tea

Evening meal: Cheese and onion savoury
Broccoli
Peas
Soaked dried or fresh banana

Bedtime: Bouillon, grape juice or slippery elm or molasses and water

Menu 3

First thing: (choice of)
Lemon and honey
Bottled apple juice
Bottled water

Breakfast: Muesli with grated raw apple and yogurt

Mid-morning: Coffee substitute e.g. Barley Cup ½ milk, ½ water

Lunch: Salad: Lettuce, cress, tomato, pepper, grated raw beetroot, celery
2 oz (50g) grated cheese
1 potato, boiled or baked
Molasses jelly and top of milk

Mid-afternoon: China or herb tea

Evening meal: Moussaka with soya or beef mince
Peas, cabbage, carrots
Baked apple

Bedtime: Grape juice or bouillon
Molasses and water

Menu 4

First thing: (Choice of)
Lemon and honey
Bottled apple juice
Bottled water

Breakfast: Prunes and yogurt with 1 tablespoonful
  ground almonds and honey

Mid-morning: Coffee substitute or fruit juice

Lunch: Salad: Celery, cooked beetroot, lettuce, dried
  pear, pepper, tomato
Hard-boiled egg
1 slice 100% wholewheat bread with butter or Ryvita
1 homemade bun

Mid-afternoon: China or herb tea or fruit juice

Evening meal: ½ grapefruit
  Cheese, tomato and lentil rissoles (or grilled fish),
  chopped parsley, celery and carrots
Baked apple

Bedtime: Grape juice or coffee substitute
  Molasses and water

Menu 5

First thing: (choice of)
Lemon and honey
Bottled apple juice

Bottled water

Breakfast: ½ grapefruit
1 pear
2 soaked dried bananas
Yogurt

Mid-morning: Coffee substitute
Fruit juice

Lunch: Salad: Lettuce or chinese leaves, tomato,
pepper, grated carrot, celery
4 oz (100g) cottage cheese
Potato
Fresh apple

Mid-afternoon: China or herb tea or fruit juice

Evening meal: ½ grapefruit
Cauliflower cheese
Tomatoes, carrots

Bedtime: Grape juice or coffee substitute
Molasses and water

Menu 6

First thing: (choice of)
Lemon and honey
Bottled apple juice
Bottled water

Breakfast: Prunes and yogurt
1-2 slices toast (100% wholewheat bread), butter,
honey or 2 Ryvitas
Mid-morning: Coffee substitute
Tomato juice

Lunch: Salad: Lettuce, tomato, grated carrot, boiled rice
with chopped mint or chives, peppers
2 oz (50g) grated cheese
Homemade cake

Mid-afternoon: Tea or fruit juice

Evening meal: Brown spaghetti with tomato sauce,
Cabbage, carrots
Fresh or baked apple

Bedtime: Grape juice or molasses and water

Menu 7

First thing: (choice of)
Lemon and honey
Bottled apple juice
Bottled water

Breakfast: ½ grapefruit
1 apple
1 peach or 8-12 grapes
Yogurt and honey

Mid-morning: Coffee substitute, or fruit juice

Lunch: Salad: Chinese leaves, pepper, cress, grated carrot, few raisins, grated apple, 2 oz. (50g) milled nuts, sunflower seeds
1 slice 100% wholewheat bread and butter
Banana (fresh or dried)

Mid-afternoon: Tea or fruit juice

Evening meal: Cheese and tomato quiche (chicken)
Peas, carrots, broccoli
Stewed or baked apple

Bedtime: Grape juice or molasses and water

Menu 8

First thing: Fruit juice

Breakfast: Bran flakes with milk and raisins
1 slice bread or toast

Mid-morning: Coffee substitute or tomato juice

Lunch: Good mixed salad with hardboiled egg
Baked rice pudding

Mid-afternoon: Tea or fruit juice

Evening meal: Vegetable and millet soup with grated cheese
Compote of dried fruits and yogurt

Bedtime: Grape juice

PROGRESSIVE RECIPES
Baked Apple

Wash and core apple, score the skin twice, place in a tin or oven proof dish in which there is just a covering of water. Insert a teaspoonful of honey in the core hole. Bake for 20-30 minutes at 400°F (204°C, gas mark 5)

Casserole of Vegetables (to serve 2)

1 small onion
1 tablespoonful of sunflower oil
1 pepper, thinly chopped
2 tomatoes, scalded and skinned
2 medium carrots, coarsely grated
2-3 sticks of celery, chopped
1 large courgette (or ⅓ cucumber), sliced
Clove garlic, crushed
¼ cabbage (shredded)
1 tablespoonful of sunflower seeds
1 mug made up 'Vecon' or 'Barmene'
(1 bare teaspoonful of Vecon dissolved in mug of hot water)

Turn on oven to 400°F (204°C, gas mark 5). First, cook the sliced onion and pepper in the sunflower oil, until onion looks transparent. Transfer to the casserole. Add the skinned tomatoes and all other ingredients. Pour over the liquor, cover and put into the oven. Cook for

30 minutes, then lower heat to 375° (194°C, gas mark 4) for another 45 minutes. Test to see if vegetables are tender. Sprinkle with a little grated cheese or ground almonds to serve.

Cheese and Onion Savoury (to serve 2)

1 small onion, sliced and chopped
3 oz (75g) grated cheddar cheese
2 oz (50g) soya flour
2 oz (50g) brown bread crumbs
2 oz (50g) brown rice flour
1 egg
2 tablespoonsful sunflower oil
½ teaspoonful of salt
½ teaspoonful of dried sage or 1 teaspoonful of fresh, chopped

Mix the flours and breadcrumbs, add salt and herbs, add onion and cheese then the oil and egg beaten together. The mixture should be a stiff dropping consistency, i.e. just dropping off the fork – but not easily. Put the mixture into a greased basin – tie down with greaseproof paper, then metal foil (or a cloth) and steam in boiling water (halfway up basin) for 1 hour.

Muesli

There is a fashion at present to use the various brands of muesli from the packet with added milk and fruit. This can be difficult to digest. The original Bircher Muesli stipulated that the oat flakes (wheat or barley or soya, as the case may be) should be soaked overnight – *then* the chopped nuts, raisins, grated raw apple and skimmed milk added with little muscavado sugar (dark brown or unrefined sugar).

Molasses Jelly

½ pint (275ml) water
2 tablespoonsful of molasses (or black treacle)
1 rounded teaspoonful of agar-agar

Bring water to the boil and dissolve molasses in it. Sprinkle in the agar and stir simmering 2-3 minutes. Remove from heat and divide into small dishes.
N.B: A little grated lemon rind can be added to the cold water before boiling, to give extra flavour.

Moussaka (serves 2)

4 oz 100g) soya natural mince (or 6 oz (175g) beef
    mince, pre-cooked)
(reconstituted in a cup of made up Bouillon plus 1
    crushed clove of garlic and ¼ teaspoonful of salt)
4 oz (100g) mushrooms, sliced
2 tomatoes scalded and skinned and sliced
3-4 medium potatoes, scrubbed well
1 teaspoonful of thyme
1 tablespoon of sunflower oil

Grease appropriate-sized oven dish or tin. Thinly slice a potato and line the dish. Pour in half the mince, add a layer of mushrooms and tomatoes and a sprinkling of thyme – another layer of thinly sliced potato – the rest of the mince with mushrooms and tomato and thyme. Finish with topping of potato and the oil. Bake in moderate oven 375°, gas mark 4 for 35-45 minutes.

Fruit Buns or Cake

2 oz (50g) soya flour
2 oz (50g) rice flour
2 oz (50g) ground almonds
2 oz (50g) 100% wholewheat flour
4 oz (100g) margarine
4 tablespoonsful sunflower oil
3 eggs
4 oz (100g) muscavado sugar
or 2 oz (50g) honey and 2 oz (50g) sugar
3-4 oz (75-100g) fruit – currants, sultanas, raisins
1 lemon, grated rind and juice

Mix together all flours and the almonds. In another bowl cream the fats together then add the sugar/honey and cream well. Add one egg at a time, plus 1 tablespoonful of flour and beat well to a light and foaming consistency. Now fold in the remaining flour, the fruit and lemon rind and juice and put into prepared bun tins or a cake tin and *either* (for buns) bake at 400°F (204°C, gas mark 5) for 15-20 minutes *or* (for cake) bake at 375° F (191°C, gas mark 4) for 1 hour

Alternative flavouring – use black treacle as sweetener, with 1 teaspoonful mixed spice instead of lemon.

Cheese, Tomato and Lentil Rissoles

4 oz (100g) red lentils, well soaked (3-4 hours)
3 oz (75g) grated cheddar cheese
3 tomatoes, scalded and skinned
1 teaspoonful tomato purée
1 teaspoonful of muscavado sugar
½ teaspoonful of salt
1-2 cloves garlic, crushed (according to taste)
1 egg
¼ teaspoonful of oregano
Bran, sunflower oil

Simmer lentils until soft, then leave to cool. Add
cheese, tomatoes, purée, sugar and salt, garlic and
oregano. Mix well together, add beaten egg to bind.
Shape into rissoles, dip into bran and dry 'fry' or grill
fairly slowly for 7 minutes each side. Add small amount
of sunflower oil to baste and prevent from sticking.
Sprinkle with chopped parsley and serve.

Cauliflower Cheese (serves 4)

Break up cauliflower into florets and par-boil 5 minutes
in slightly salted water. Remove and drain and pile into
oven dish with sauce and bake 15-20 minutes at 375°F
(191°C, gas mark 4).

Sauce
½ pint (275ml) milk
Pat of butter

1 tablespoonful of brown rice flour
3 oz (75g) of cheddar cheese, grated
Breadcrumbs or bran to top

Heat milk and butter, stir in rice flour. Bring to boil and cook 3 minutes. Remove from heat and mix in cheese. Pour over cauliflower, sprinkle over crumbs or bran and bake.

Cheese and Tomato Quiche

Pastry is used in this recipe – but if it appears on the menu only once in a week it should be tolerated. Made with these wholesome ingredients it makes less demands on the digestion.

2 oz (50g) 100% wholewheat flour
2 oz (50g) rice flour 100%
1 oz (25g) cheddar cheese grated
2-3 tablespoonsful of sunflower oil
Water to mix

Mix the flours in a bowl. Add the grated cheese. Mix in the oil with a knife and then with a wire pastry blender. Add water to mix to a stiff dough. Prepare small flan tin. Collect dough into a ball and put onto floured board. 'Knuckle' it down to required size and thickness to line flan tin (this is better than rolling).

Filling
3-4 tomatoes according to size
3 oz (75g) cheddar cheese, grated

2 eggs
½ pint milk
Clove garlic

Scald and skin tomatoes. Slice into the flan and cover with cheese. Beat eggs in milk with crushed garlic. Pour over tomatoes and cheese – but not to overflow!

Bake in fairly hot oven at 425°F (218°C, gas mark 6) for 20 minutes. Lower heat to 400°F (204°C, gas mark 5) for 10-15 minutes. If not quite set allow another 5 minutes with lower heat still.

Baked Rice Pudding

3 level tablespoonsful of brown rice (well washed)
1 pint (550ml) milk
2 tablespoonsful (level) of honey or dark sugar

The dark sugar tends to curdle the milk so this pudding needs to be cooked very slowly.

Blend all ingredients together and bake at 300°F (149°C, gas mark 1-2) for 2½ hours.

Of further interest

RECIPES FOR HEALTH:
IRRITABLE BOWEL SYNDROME

Jill Davies and Ann Page Wood

Irritable Bowel Syndrome, or IBS, is a very common bowel disorder which accounts for over 50 per cent of referrals to gastro-intestinal clinics. What you eat is of great importance in helping to control this condition.

Specialists usually advise a high-fibre diet – and many sufferers benefit from a diet low in fat and high in protein.

This practical guide can be used in conjunction with your doctor's treatment. The authors:

- explain what is meant by the term 'irritable bowel syndrome'
- discuss the various physical and psychological factors associated with the disorder
- give guidelines on coping with IBS

The tempting recipes are based on cereals, fruit and vegetables, and high-protein foods. The amount of fibre is given in each dish.

With this book, you can help yourself to better health and learn to cope with and even overcome your IBS.

IRRITABLE BOWEL SYNDROME & DIVERTICULOSIS

A SELF-HELP PLAN

Shirley Trickett

Half the people who consult gastroenterologists with bowel problems are diagnosed as having Irritable Bowel Syndrome. Their symptoms vary – from chronic constipation to chronic diarrhoea, abdominal pains, colic, headaches and backache – and very often conventional treatment, such as high-fibre diets or drugs, makes matters worse. So, what exactly is IBS, and how can sufferers help themselves?

In straightforward style, Shirley Trickett explains the exact nature of the range of symptoms described as IBS, and what causes them. The effects of associated conditions such as Candidiasis, ME, food allergies and addictions are described, and she provides practical suggestions for action in each case.

She then details a range of self-help therapies which can be of enormous benefit, including dietary changes, relaxation therapies, physical exercise and breathing techniques. Finally, the various approaches of several complementary therapies of proven benefit to bowel disorders – homoeopathy, therapeutic massage, colonic irrigation, reflexology, shiatsu and aromatherapy – are described by experts in each field.

BANISH ANXIETY

A COMMON-SENSE PLAN FOR REGAINING CONTROL OF YOUR LIFE

Dr Kenneth Hambly

Do you feel anxious about work, your social life or even shopping?

It is perfectly normal and natural to react to difficult situations by becoming anxious. But do you feel you worry too much about things that you want to be able to cope with? Are you anxious all of the time? Do you experience excessive anxiety in difficult situations?

Dr Kenneth Hambly recognises that suffering from anxiety limits your life and prevents you from enjoying it to the full. He proposes a common-sense action plan for dealing with it and recovering from it.

By following Dr Hambly's advice, sufferers can regain a happier, healthier life and need never feel trapped by anxiety again.

STRESS

PROVEN STRESS-COPING STRATEGIES FOR BETTER HEALTH

Leon Chaitow

Do you suffer from migraine, chronic back pain, frequent colds, fatigue, panic attacks or high blood pressure? If so, too much stress could be damaging your health.

Stress has a disastrous effect on our immune systems, and can be the major cause of both mild and serious health problems. Psychoneuroimmunology, or PNI, is the science which holds the key to many common health problems. It points to new ways to control these damaging emotions and so protect our bodies' natural defences and ward off illness.

Leading health writer Leon Chaitow here uses the latest research into the mind/body connection to help you create your own stress protection plan. Advice on diet, exercise, meditation, relaxation, guided imagery and visualization, with useful checklists, will help you develop your own system to cope with the inevitable pressures of life.

Leon Chaitow, naturopath and acupuncturist, is a leading international practitioner and successful author of a wide range of health books.

HEALING THROUGH NUTRITION

A NATURAL APPROACH TO TREATING 50 COMMON ILLNESSES WITH DIET AND NUTRIENTS

Dr Melvyn R. Werbach

This indispensable reference book provides the nutritional roots of and treatments for 50 common illnesses, from allergies and the common cold to cancer.

The world's authority on the relationship between nutrition and illness, Dr Melvyn Werbach makes it easy to learn what you can do to influence the course of your health via the nutrients that you feed your body.

A chapter is devoted to each of the 50 ailments and this highly accessible A–Z of nutritional health includes:

- an analysis of dietary factors affecting health and well-being
- a suggested healing diet for 50 common illnesses
- nutritional healing plans, with recommended dosages for vitamins, minerals and other essential nutrients
- an explanation of vitamin supplements and how they can improve your health

There are also guidelines on how to plan the right healing diet for yourself and how to diagnose food sensitivities. With this groundbreaking guide you will be able to make informed decisions about the essential role of nutrients in your health and well-being.

RECIPES FOR HEALTH: IRRITABLE BOWEL SYNDROME	0 7225 3141 9	£5.99	☐
IRRITABLE BOWEL SYNDROME & DIVERTICULOSIS	0 7225 2401 3	£5.99	☐
BANISH ANXIETY	0 7225 3112 5	£5.99	☐
STRESS	0 7225 3192 3	£5.99	☐
HEALING THROUGH NUTRITION	0 7225 2941 5	£16.99	☐

All these books are available from your local bookseller or can be ordered direct from the publishers.

To order direct just tick the titles you want and fill in the form below:

Name: _____

Address: _____

_____

_____ Postcode: _____

Send to: Thorsons Mail Order, Dept 3, HarperCollins*Publishers*, Westerhill Road, Bishopbriggs, Glasgow G64 2QT.
Please enclose a cheque or postal order or your authority to debit your Visa/Access account –

Credit card no: _____

Expiry date: _____

Signature: _____

– to the value of the cover price plus:
UK & BFPO: Add £1.00 for the first book and 25p for each additional book ordered.
Overseas orders including Eire: Please add £2.95 service charge. Books will be sent by surface mail but quotes for airmail despatches will be given on request.

24 HOUR TELEPHONE ORDERING SERVICE FOR ACCESS/VISA CARDHOLDERS – **TEL: 0141 772 2281.**